15A1

D1741271

JUST LOOK AT...
THE CHANGING EARTH

Keith Lye

Macdonald Educational

Factual Adviser: Dr Alan Woolley

Editor: Barbara Tombs
Teacher Panel: Tim Firth,
David Rowbotham, Hazel Stimpson
Designer: Ewing Paddock
Production: Rosemary Bishop
Picture Research: Kathy Lockley

Illustrations
Mike Atkinson 14–15, 18–19, 20, 22–23, 24–25,
27, 28-29
Peter Dennis/Linda Rogers Associates 32–33,
34–35, 36–37, 38–39
Kevin Maddison Cover cartoon, 8, 17, 31, 33, 42
Lee Montgomery 10–11, 12, 40–41

Photographs
Ardea/I. R. Beames, 13T; /Wardene Weisser, 29,
35T
British Trust for Conservation Volunteers, 41T
Bruce Coleman/G. D. Plage, 13B; /Jane Burton,
16–17
Mary Evans Picture Library, 26
Geological Society, 16
Geoscience Features, 14, 15
Robert Harding Picture Library, 11T, 24–25, 27,
35B, 39B
Frank Lane Agency, 8, 20–21, 25B, 30
Marion and Tony Morrison, 39T
Frank Spooner Pictures, Cover
United States Geological Survey/R. E. Wallace
(40), 22
Zefa Picture Library, Title page, 11B, 28–29, 33,
41B, 43

Title page photo: Stalactites and stalagmites.
Back cover cartoon: Earthquake caused by the
twitching of a giant frog. (Mongolian story.)

British Library Cataloguing in Publication Data
Lye, Keith
    The changing earth. – (Just look at)
    1. Earth – Juvenile literature
    I. Title   II. Series
    550   QE29
    ISBN 0-356-11182-2

How to use this book

Look first in the contents page to see if the subject you want is listed. For instance, if you want to find out about volcanoes you will find the information on pages 24 and 25. The word list explains the more difficult terms found in this book. The index will tell you how many times a particular subject is mentioned and whether there is a picture of it.

The Changing Earth is one of a series of books about Our World. All the books on this subject have a blue band around the cover. If you want to know more about the world about us and our bodies, look for other books with a blue band in the **Just Look At . . .** series.

© Macdonald & Co. (Publishers) Ltd. 1985

First published in Great Britain in 1985
by Macdonald & Co. (Publishers) Ltd.
London & Sydney

Printed and bound in Great Britain by Purnell & Sons
(Book Production) Ltd., Paulton, nr. Bristol.

Macdonald & Co. (Publishers) Ltd.
Maxwell House, 74 Worship Street, London EC2A 2EN

Members of BPCC plc. *All rights reserved.*

CONTENTS

Studying Our Planet   8–19

The Changing Landscape   10–11
Ice, Wind and Sea   12–13
How Rocks are Formed   14–15
The Meaning of Fossils   16–17
The Story of the Earth   18–19

The Restless Earth   20–29

Moving Continents   22–23
Volcanoes   24–25
Earthquakes   26–27
Mountain Building   28–29

Weather   30–35

Weather Forecasting   32–33
Changing Climates   34–35

Life on Earth   36–41

Interfering with Nature   38–39
Looking after our Planet   40–41

Books, Places and Records   42–43
Word List and Index   44–45

STUDYING OUR PLANET

Our planet Earth is home for a great variety of living things. The Earth is the third planet from the Sun in the Solar System. This means that the Sun keeps the Earth warm. But it does not overheat our planet. By contrast, Mercury and Venus, the two planets closest to the Sun are extremely hot. On Mars, the fourth planet from the Sun, temperatures are always below freezing point. Only the Earth can support living things as we know them.

Today we are able to study colour pictures of our planet home taken from space. The pictures show us that the Earth is round, not flat as most people once thought. The blue on the photographs is water, because oceans cover more than seven-tenths of the Earth's surface. The rest is land. Above the land and the oceans are swirling white clouds. The clouds remind us that a thin layer of air, called the atmosphere, surrounds the Earth. Without the atmosphere, we would not be able to breathe.

The oceans, the atmosphere and even the land are constantly moving and changing. Some changes to the land are slow, for instance the way continents are moved by powerful forces inside the Earth. The sea, rivers, glaciers and the weather all work to change the Earth slowly.

Changes caused by earthquakes and volcanic eruptions are often violent and sudden. In a few minutes, they can destroy cities and kill many people. People have suggested many ideas to explain such changes. Hawaiian legends told of the goddess Pele, who caused earthquakes by stamping her foot. When she was angry she brought molten rock called lava to the surface to destroy anyone who had upset her. In 1716, a French writer said that lava was formed when the fat of animals, drowned in the Biblical flood, caught fire inside the Earth.

No one believes these ideas today. But there are still unsolved mysteries about the Earth and how it changes. Some of the problems that scientists are now studying are concerned with what people are doing to the Earth. For example, when people farm the world's grasslands, they expose the soil to the wind. The wind may blow the dry soil away and the land may become a desert. People also harm the Earth by polluting and poisoning the land, air and water. To prevent serious damage to our Earth, we must study how and why it changes and what happens when we interfere with nature.

▲ The Romans thought that volcanoes erupted when the blacksmith god Vulcan was hard at work in his forge.

An earthquake damaged many houses in Anchorage, Alaska, in 1964 and killed 115 people.

The Changing Landscape

At night in hot deserts, you may hear sounds like pistol shots. These sounds occur when rocks which have been heated during the day cool quickly after sunset. Because they cool so quickly, the surface of the rock cracks, and gradually layers of rock peel away like the layers of an onion. This is one example of how the weather can change the land. We call this action mechanical weathering.

Another type of mechanical weathering, the work of frost, occurs in cold, wet regions. Water collects in the cracks of rocks during the day. This water freezes at night. When water turns to ice it expands and takes up more space than the same amount of water. So when water freezes, the ice pushes against both sides of the cracks. The cracks become wider until the rocks split apart. The broken rocks then tumble downhill and pile up in heaps called scree or talus.

Chemical weathering

Water also weathers rocks. For example, pure water dissolves some substances, such as rock salt from which we get some of our household salt. This is an example of chemical weathering.

Rainwater also weathers limestone, a common, hard rock often used in building. Limestone rocks in the ground are split by a network of vertical and horizontal cracks. Rainwater seeps through these cracks and slowly widens them. It wears out deep holes in the ground which plunge downwards to a dark maze of tunnels and underground chambers.

The world's biggest caves all occur in limestone rocks. People called pot-holers enjoy exploring them. Water flowing through limestone caves often reappears on the surface as springs. Springs are the sources of many rivers.

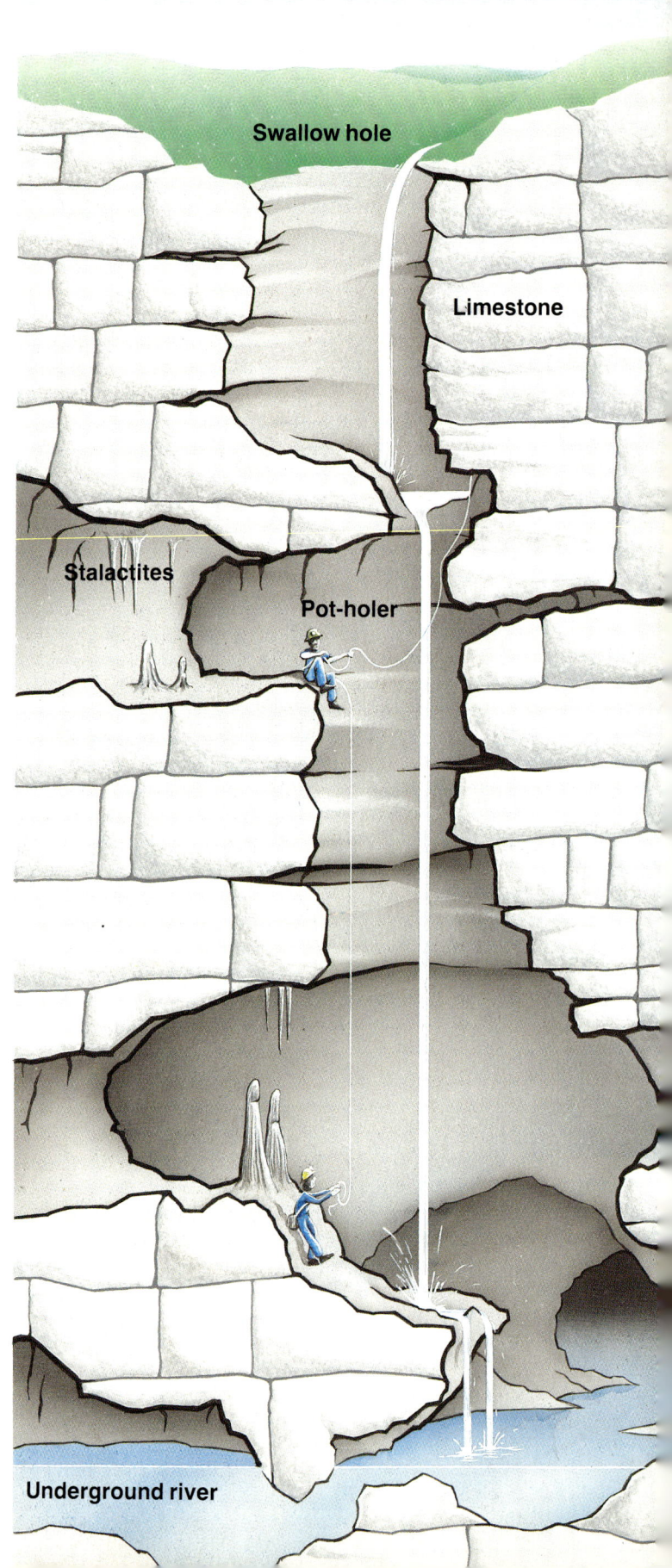

Swallow hole

Limestone

Stalactites

Pot-holer

Underground river

The work of rivers

Rivers are also important in changing the Earth's surface. They wash loose rocks downhill, which scrape along the bottom of the river bed, loosening other rocks. This is how rivers deepen and widen their valleys. The rocks rub against each other and break down into tiny pieces called silt or mud. Rivers nearing the sea contain a lot of this material.

Scientists estimate that the Mississippi River in the USA carries more than 440 million tonnes of silt to the sea every year. This silt comes from the Mississippi River basin. They have also worked out that about one metre of land is removed from all of North America every 30,000 years. This may sound slow. But over millions of years, weathering and rivers can wear down the highest mountains to flat plains.

▲ Beautiful carvings on the walls of many old churches, such as Chartres Cathedral, France, are slowly worn away by weathering.

Most rivers flow into the sea through estuaries. They look muddy, because they contain large amounts of fine sediment. ▼

Most large caves occur in areas of limestone rocks. Rainwater slowly wears away the limestone along vertical and horizontal cracks in the hard rock.

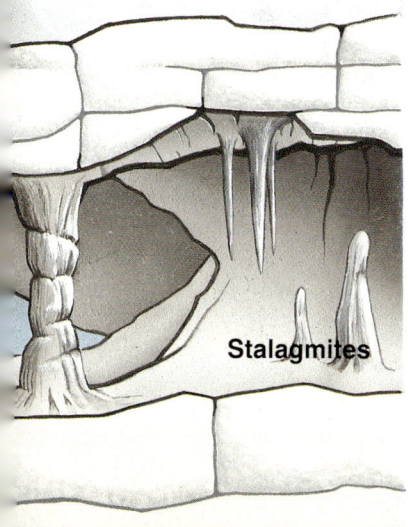

Stalagmites

Ice, Wind and Sea

The wind, sea and moving rivers of ice, called glaciers, also change the land. Glaciers are found in mountains. They form in hollows called cirques, where snow piles up year after year. The snow is gradually pressed into solid ice. Eventually the ice starts to move away from the cirques down valleys. Rocks on the bottom of the ice scrape against the land. They prise away rocks and carve out deep, U-shaped valleys.

Like a huge bulldozer, the glacier pushes along rocks of all shapes and sizes. These rocks are called moraine. Moraine is dropped at the end, or snout, of the glaciers to form hills and ridges, or swept away by streams of melted ice.

Large boulders, called erratics, have been found in ice-free parts of central Europe and the USA.

The diagram shows a mountain region which has been eroded by glaciers. Deep, U-shaped valleys, waterfalls and jagged peaks called horns are typical features. ▼

These boulders may be made of rocks of a different type from those beneath them. Ice sheets carried them to their present positions thousands of years ago during the Ice Age.

The work of winds

Winds shape the land in desert regions. Strong winds blow sand across the land. Near the ground, this wind-blown sand acts much like a sand-blaster used in cities to clean dirty buildings. It wears caves in cliffs and undercuts boulders so that they look like tall mushrooms standing on narrow stems.

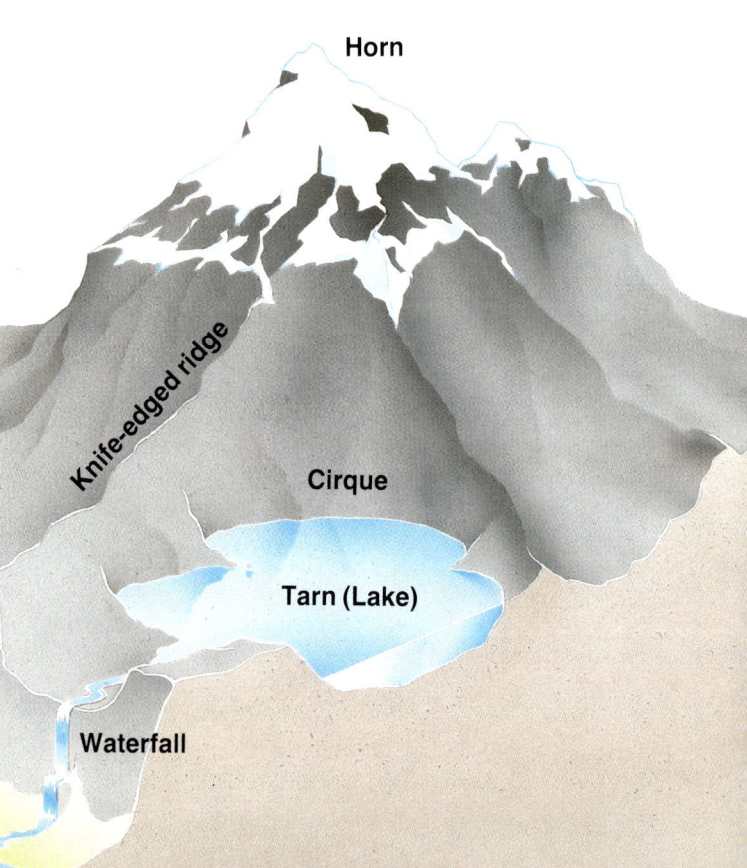

Horn

Knife-edged ridge

Cirque

Hanging valley

Tarn (Lake)

U-shaped valley

Waterfall

Loose sand is sometimes blown into hills called dunes. Dunes are always on the move and they sometimes threaten farms. Drifting sand dunes may bury the fields around oases, or waterholes, in deserts. Grasses and trees are often planted in moving dunes in order to anchor them.

The work of the sea

Sea waves seem harmless on fine days. But storm waves carrying pebbles and rocks batter sea cliffs and wear out caves. Storm waves remove soft rocks faster than hard ones. Deep bays are found where soft rocks occur on the coast. Harder rocks form headlands. Even tough headlands are finally worn away. Sea waves may cut caves into both sides of a headland. The caves often meet to form arches, which finally collapse. The part of the headland which is left standing is a little rocky island called a stack, which itself will one day be worn away.

Waves and currents carry sand and pebbles out to sea or along the coast. In places, ridges of sand and pebbles are piled up by the waves. These ridges are called spits or bars.

▲ Storm waves pound this coast near the south-western tip of Portugal. The waves hollow out caves.

Wind-blown sand is undercutting this rock in Arizona, USA. Eventually, the rock will topple over. ▼

How Rocks are Formed

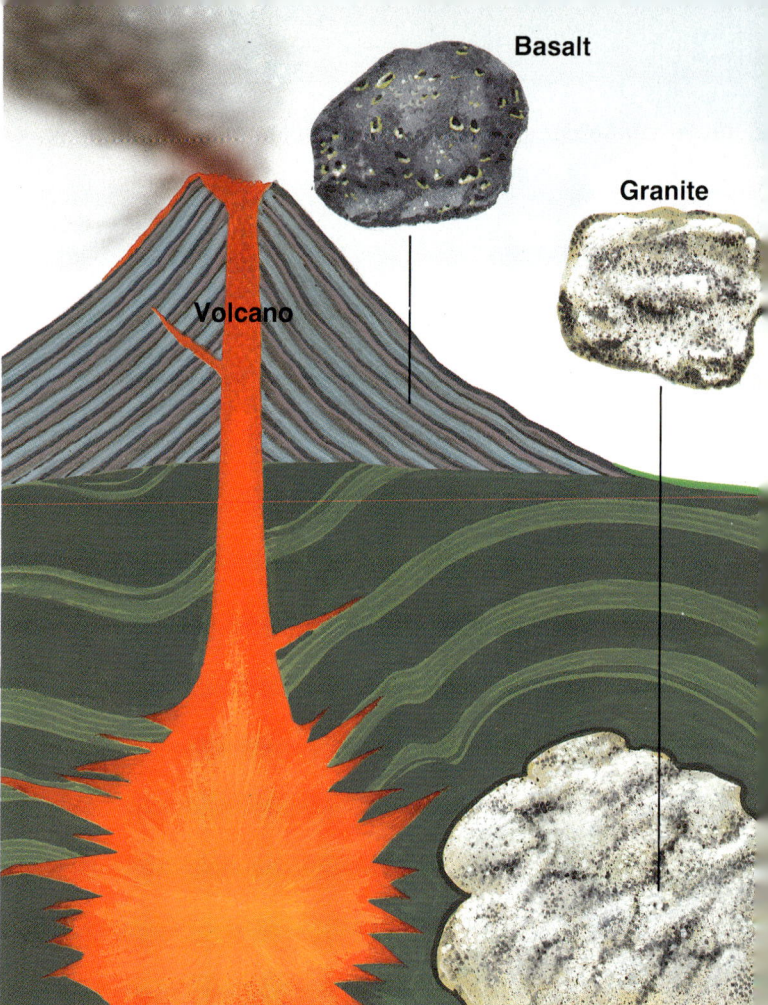

Rocks are made up of minerals, the building blocks of planet Earth. We often think that rocks are hard and heavy. But soil and mud are also rocks. Much of the material, or sediment, which has been broken up by weathering and carried by rivers, glaciers, winds and sea waves, ends up on the beds of lakes or seas. There it piles up, layer upon layer.

These layers are gradually pressed together. Water seeping through them leaves behind various minerals which act like cement and stick the loose grains together. In this way, the layers are slowly turned into solid rock. These rocks are called sedimentary rocks. But not all rocks are formed in this way. There are also two other types of rocks, called igneous and metamorphic rocks.

Igneous rocks

Igneous rocks are formed from hot molten rock called magma, which is found inside the Earth. When magma reaches the surface through volcanoes, it is called lava. A rock formed from lava when it has cooled and hardened is basalt. It is normally dark grey or black.

When a volcano explodes, the magma is broken into small pieces, called volcanic dust or ash. These fragments pile up in layers to form a rock called tuff. Other rocks formed by volcanoes are pumice, which is a light rock containing lots of holes once filled by gases, and obsidian, or volcanic glass.

Sometimes magma doesn't reach the surface but cools and hardens underground. An example of a rock which is formed in this way is granite. We find it on the surface only after the rocks which once covered it have been worn away, many thousands of years later.

This ignimbrite quarry is in Mexico. Ignimbrite is an igneous rock, made of magma exploded from a volcano. ▼

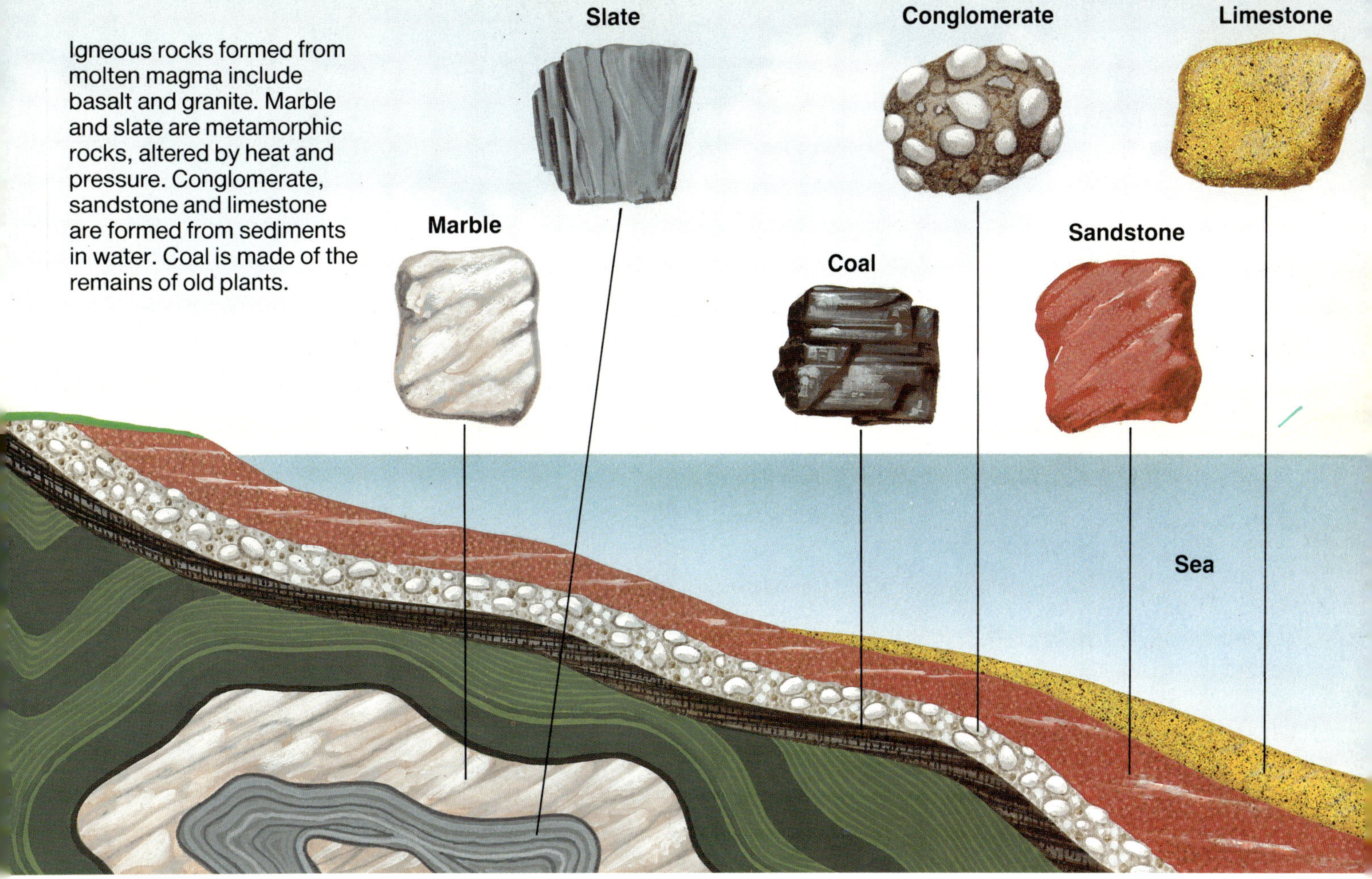

Igneous rocks formed from molten magma include basalt and granite. Marble and slate are metamorphic rocks, altered by heat and pressure. Conglomerate, sandstone and limestone are formed from sediments in water. Coal is made of the remains of old plants.

Slate

Conglomerate

Limestone

Marble

Coal

Sandstone

Sea

The buildings in this Mexican village are made of ignimbrite, which came from the quarry on the opposite page. ▼

Sedimentary rocks

Sedimentary rocks include siltstones, mudstones and shales, formed from fine silt, mud or clay. Conglomerates have pebbles cemented in silt or sand. Sandstone is formed from grains of sand.

Limestone, a common sedimentary rock, is created in several ways. For instance, some limestones consist of the remains of sea animals, such as shells, which pile up on deep sea beds. Coal is also a sedimentary rock. It consists of plant remains which have been pressed together.

Metamorphic rocks

Heat and pressure can change, or alter, rocks. This is rather like the changes that occur when wet dough is baked and turned into bread. The heat often comes from magma inside the Earth's crust. The pressure may occur during movements inside the Earth.

Altered rocks are called metamorphic rocks. They include marble, which was formerly limestone, and hard slate, used on roofs. Slate was formerly the soft rock, shale.

The Meaning of Fossils

Fossils are the evidence of plants and animals which once lived on Earth. They are found in sedimentary rocks. Some consist of the actual bodies of animals. For example, woolly mammoths which lived in the Ice Age have been found in the frozen soil of Siberia. Such fossils are rare. Bones and the impressions of other hard parts of animals are much more common.

How fossils are formed

For a fossil to form, an animal or plant must be buried quickly. This normally happens on the beds of rivers, lakes or seas. The soft parts of a buried body soon decay, leaving only the hard parts, such as the shell, or bones. These parts are pressed into the sediments, which eventually become sedimentary rocks.

As water seeps through these rocks, it often dissolves the hard parts of the buried body, creating holes or moulds of the original shape. Sometimes water leaves behind minerals in the moulds, and so creates a fossil cast. Petrified logs consisted originally of wood, but each tiny cell in the wood has been replaced by minerals and the wood has slowly turned to stone. Petrified logs are an exact copy of the original. They even show the tree rings. Coal is made up of the remains of plants growing in swampy forests. Lumps of coal often contain beautiful impressions of the leaves and stems of these plants.

Footprints can also become fossilized. This happened when an animal walked across a muddy surface. The Sun baked the mud hard, preserving the footprints. The mud was then covered and slowly buried by fresh sediments. These in turn became sedimentary rocks. Millions of years later, when the overlying rocks have been worn away, the footprints are exposed again.

▲ Mary Anning, a carpenter's daughter, was a great early fossil hunter.

This fossil is what remains of a fish which lived about 50 million years ago. In the Middle Ages, many Europeans thought that fossils were half-made animals left over at the Creation. ▼

What fossils mean

Scientists in ancient Greece understood that fossils were the remains of animal and plant life. But when the Greeks became less powerful, many of their ideas were forgotten. One explanation of fossils was that they were plants and animals killed in a prehistoric flood. But fossils occur in many layers of rock, one on top of another. This means they could not have been formed by one single event. Instead, as we now know, they must have been formed over an extremely long period of time.

Why fossils are important

The two scientists who founded the modern study of fossils were Frenchmen, living at the end of the 18th century. One, Jean Lamarck, became a naturalist after ill health made him leave the army. The other was a zoologist named Baron Georges Cuvier. They both classified many plant and animal fossils.

However, not all fossil experts were scientists. For instance, Mary Anning, who was born in Lyme Regis in England in 1799, did not study geology at school. But she discovered the first fossil Plesiosaur (a marine reptile) and the first Pterosaur (a flying reptile). Even today, amateurs are important. For example, a British fossil hunter found the huge claw of an unknown dinosaur as recently as 1982.

But fossils do not only provide us with valuable information about the story of life on Earth. They are also extremely important in helping us to find out the age of rocks. This is because many species lived only a short time before they became extinct. As a result, all layers of rock which contain the same fossils of a short-lived species are of the same age.

The Story of the Earth

Armed with an iron file, you might be able to scrape away 5 millimetres of rock from a lump of limestone in 10 minutes. But natural weathering is taking 100 years to remove 5 millimetres from the limestone walls of St Paul's Cathedral in London. So slow is this process that it would take 20,000 years to wear away a 1 metre thick wall. But even 20,000 years is a brief moment in Earth history. Compare it with the age of the limestone used to build St Paul's. This rock formed on a sea bed in the Jurassic period, between 190 and 136 million years ago.

The actual age of the Earth has been disputed over the years, but scientists can now measure the ages of rocks more accurately. They estimate that the Earth is about 4,600 million years old. To help us understand Earth history, geologists have divided it into eras, like chapters in a book. The eras are split into periods, and some periods are divided into epochs and ages. The first era, Chapter 1, lasts from 4,600 to 570 million years ago. We know little about life on Earth at that time. Rocks formed then contain very few fossils because most creatures had soft bodies and decayed easily.

Imagine all of Earth history compressed into one day. On this scale, microscopic organisms probably appear first at 4 am. But the first animals with backbones, fishes, do not appear until 9.20 pm. Man-like apes appear 1 minute before midnight and modern people less than 1 second before midnight. ▶

Early land plants

Ichthyostega **(an early amphibian)**

Dimetrodon **(an early reptile)**

Early time

Archaeopteryx **(the first bird)**

Stegosaurus **(a dinosaur)**

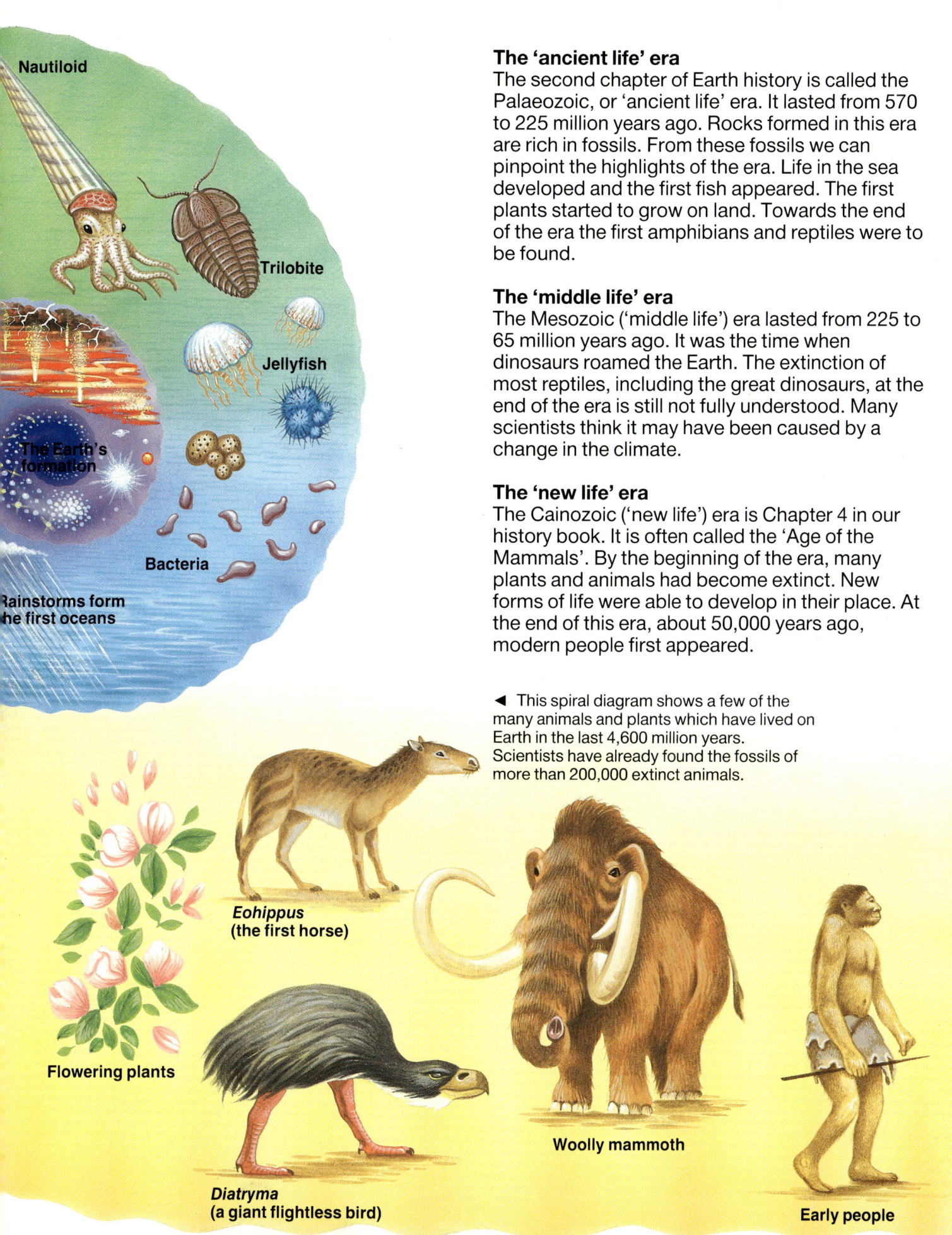

Nautiloid

Trilobite

Jellyfish

The Earth's formation

Bacteria

Rainstorms form the first oceans

The 'ancient life' era

The second chapter of Earth history is called the Palaeozoic, or 'ancient life' era. It lasted from 570 to 225 million years ago. Rocks formed in this era are rich in fossils. From these fossils we can pinpoint the highlights of the era. Life in the sea developed and the first fish appeared. The first plants started to grow on land. Towards the end of the era the first amphibians and reptiles were to be found.

The 'middle life' era

The Mesozoic ('middle life') era lasted from 225 to 65 million years ago. It was the time when dinosaurs roamed the Earth. The extinction of most reptiles, including the great dinosaurs, at the end of the era is still not fully understood. Many scientists think it may have been caused by a change in the climate.

The 'new life' era

The Cainozoic ('new life') era is Chapter 4 in our history book. It is often called the 'Age of the Mammals'. By the beginning of the era, many plants and animals had become extinct. New forms of life were able to develop in their place. At the end of this era, about 50,000 years ago, modern people first appeared.

◄ This spiral diagram shows a few of the many animals and plants which have lived on Earth in the last 4,600 million years. Scientists have already found the fossils of more than 200,000 extinct animals.

Eohippus
(the first horse)

Flowering plants

Diatryma
(a giant flightless bird)

Woolly mammoth

Early people

THE RESTLESS EARTH

People used to believe that earthquakes and volcanic eruptions were the work of gods. For example, Fijians believed that the Earth shook when a god named Ngendei, who supported the Earth, moved. And in ancient Greece, the god Poseidon was held to be the cause of earthquakes. The Greeks thought that Poseidon could split mountains and use the pieces to make new islands.

The modern study of the restless Earth owes much to a German scientist, Alfred Wegener. He collected information about similar rocks and fossils in the various continents. He discovered that fossils of a Triassic reptile named *Lystrosaurus* were to be found in Africa, India and Antarctica. These animals could not have swum from Africa to Antarctica. One way to explain this puzzle was that Africa, India and Antarctica were once joined together. Wegener argued that, 200 million years ago, all the continents were linked together. This huge supercontinent later broke up. The pieces then slowly drifted by an average of 1–2 centimetres a year to their present positions.

In the last 40 years, scientists have discovered much evidence to explain how this slow movement, or continental drift, occurs. Their discoveries also help to explain why earthquakes and volcanic eruptions occur, and how mountains are formed.

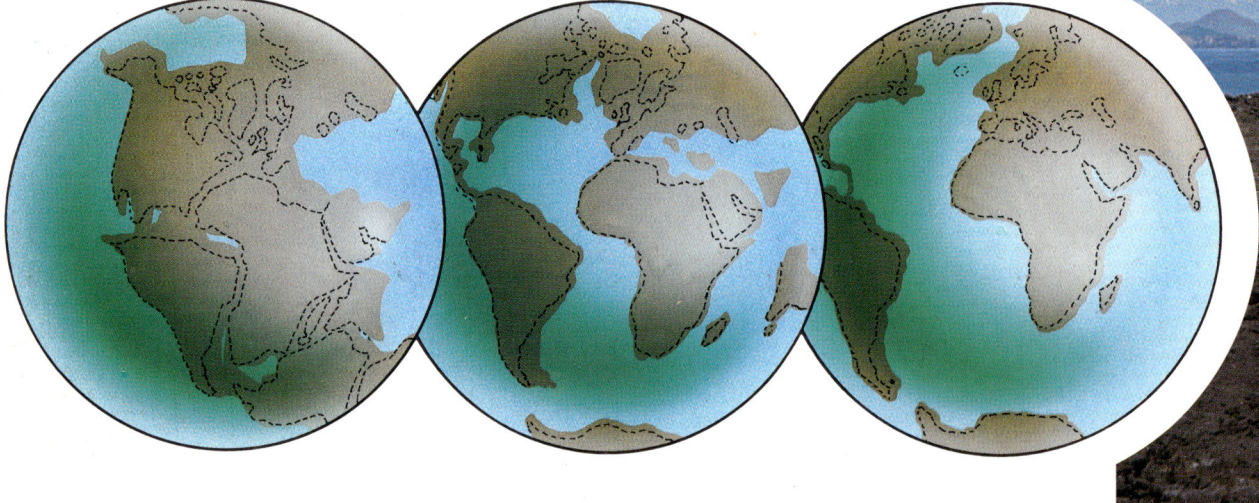

▲ A view of our Earth 200 million years ago. At that time, there was only one large continent. It was called Pangaea.

Continental drift broke up the large continent. The other globes show the Earth 60 million years ago and today.

Moving Continents

The study of the oceans in the last 40 years has helped to prove Wegener's ideas about continental drift. Beneath the oceans, there are large flat plains, volcanic peaks and huge mountain ranges called ocean ridges. The deepest parts of the oceans are trenches near continents or chains of islands.

Ocean ridges

Scientists have taken rock samples from the ocean ridges. They have found that the youngest rocks were in the centre and that rocks get older and older away from the ridges in both directions. The oldest rocks were nearly all less than 200 million years old. This proved that oceans were much younger than continents, where rocks up to 3,800 million years old have been found. Earthquakes and volcanoes are common along the ocean ridges.

Ocean trenches

Earthquakes and volcanoes are also common near the deep ocean trenches. The scientists argued that the ridges and trenches are unstable, or changing, parts of the Earth. They suggested that there are breaks in the Earth's crust along the ridges and trenches, like cracks in an eggshell. Between the cracks are large, unbroken areas which are mostly stable. The scientists called the unbroken areas 'plates'.

The plates are around 100 kilometres thick. They consist of the Earth's crust and part of the upper mantle. The mantle is the part of the Earth between the crust and the core. It is about 2,900 kilometres thick. The continents are part of the crust. They rest on the plates like ships frozen in polar ice. Just as ships frozen in ice move about, carried by ocean currents, so continents also drift when currents in the mantle move the plates.

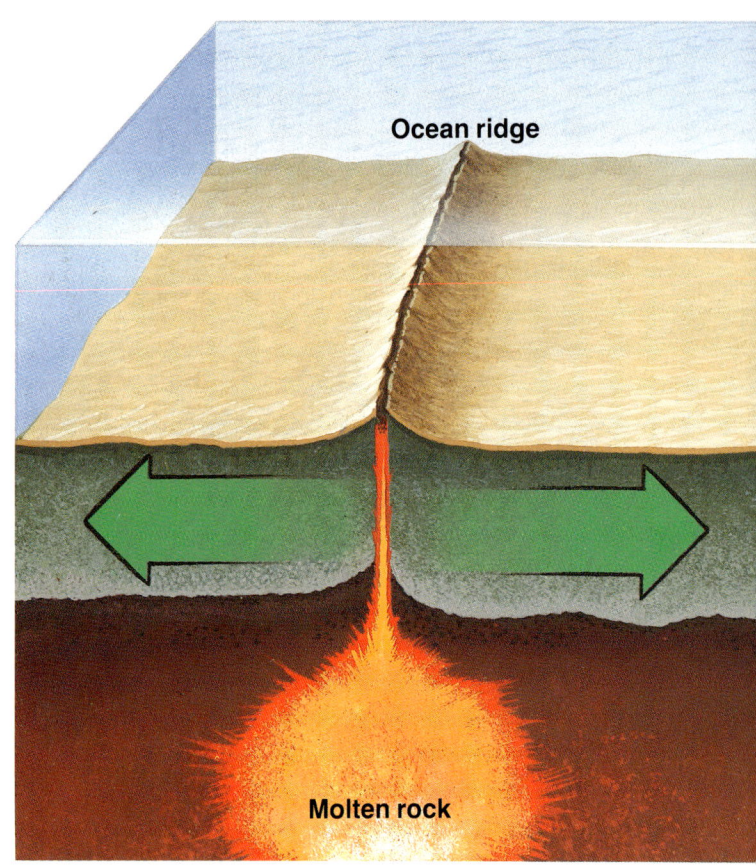

Ocean ridge

Molten rock

◄ The San Andreas fault is a long crack in the Earth's crust. The map below shows the position of the San Andreas fault. It cuts across California in south-western USA.

North America

Plates move apart along ocean ridges, and new crustal rock fills the gaps. When two plates collide, one plate is pushed under the other and is melted. ▼

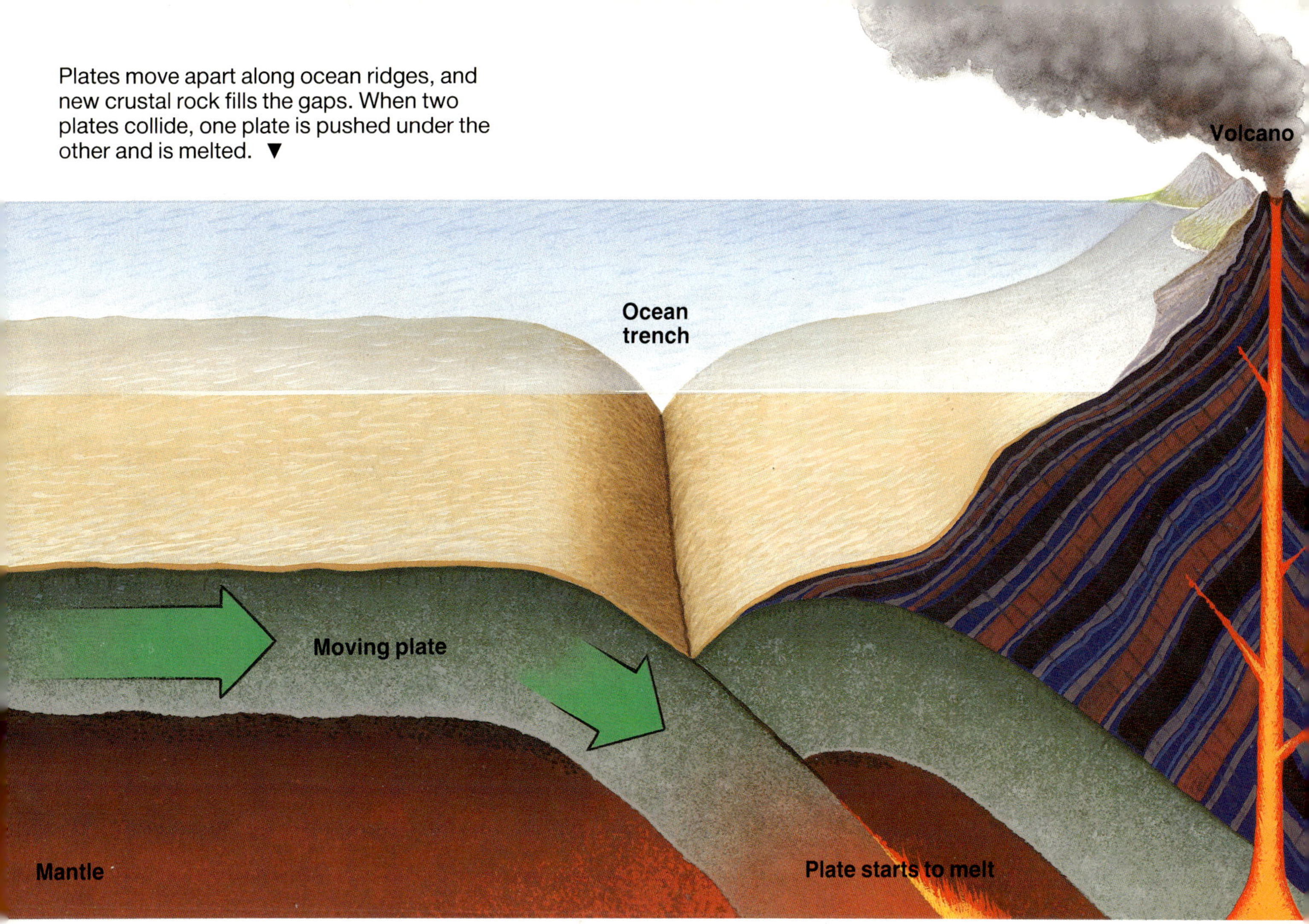

Volcano

Ocean trench

Moving plate

Mantle

Plate starts to melt

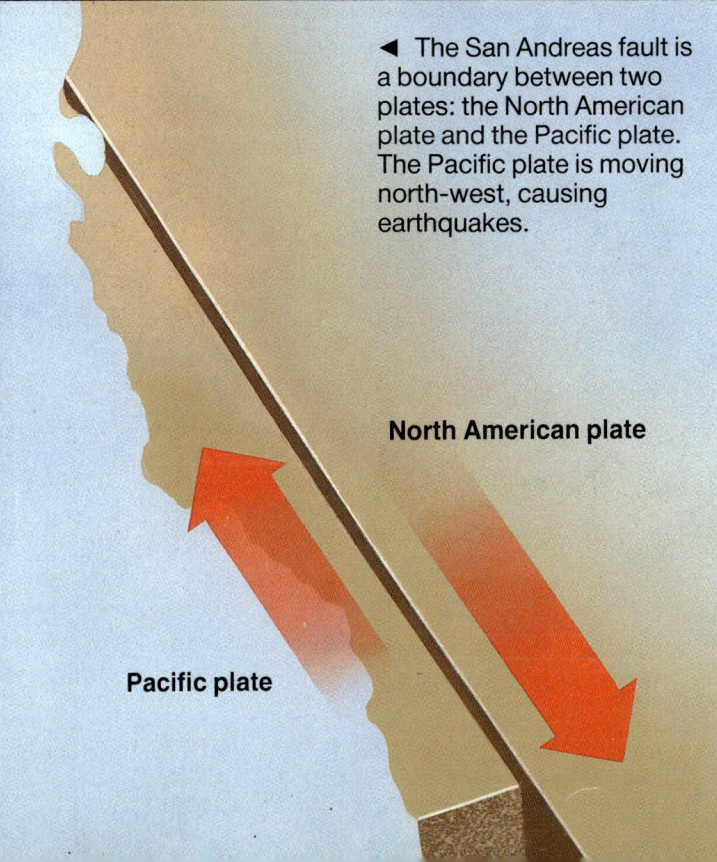

◄ The San Andreas fault is a boundary between two plates: the North American plate and the Pacific plate. The Pacific plate is moving north-west, causing earthquakes.

North American plate

Pacific plate

How plates move

At the ocean ridges the plates are being pushed apart by the currents in the mantle. Hot, molten magma rises to fill the gaps, which then cools and hardens to form a new sea bed. This is happening in the middle of the Atlantic Ocean, where the mid-Atlantic ridge has formed.

The opposite is happening in the ocean trenches. Here, crustal rock is being destroyed. This is because two plates are pressing against each other and one is forced beneath the other. As one plate slides under the other, it starts to melt. This creates magma which rises upwards to fuel volcanoes as in Japan and Indonesia.

Transform faults

We have seen how some plates move apart and some push against each other. Other plates move sideways, alongside each other. The plates are separated by cracks in the Earth's crust, called transform faults. An example is the San Andreas fault in California, in the USA.

Volcanoes

Imagine the air thick with suffocating ash and dust, a whole forest completely flattened, 300 homes destroyed and large areas of farmland burned. This is just part of the picture of damage and havoc caused when Mount St Helens suddenly erupted on 18 May 1980, killing 60 people and 2 million animals, birds and fish.

Scientists had been keeping a close watch on the sleeping, or dormant, volcano since 1969. They were given some warning that something was about to happen when an earthquake cracked the top of the mountain in March 1980. Melted snow seeped into the cracks and turned into steam. The steam caused an explosion, which left a crater, or hole, in the mountain.

Then, at 8.32 am on 18 May, the volcano erupted. The whole of the upper part of the mountain began to slide away and a cloud of thick black ash and smoke exploded into the air. You can see the different stages of the eruption in the diagram on the right. Within a short period of time, this beautiful mountain had become more like a lifeless lunar landscape.

Volcanic magma

The magma in Mount St Helens is formed as the small Juan de Fuca plate in the Pacific Ocean slides down under the large North American plate. Many volcanoes get their magma from melting plate edges. But some, such as those in Hawaii, lie far from plate edges. Here, the magma is created by isolated sources of heat in the mantle called hotspots. When Hawaii's volcanoes erupt, they do not explode. Instead, they send out red hot rivers of runny lava. Explosive volcanoes contain pasty lava which is thick and sticky. Gases and steam which are trapped in the thick magma cause the explosions.

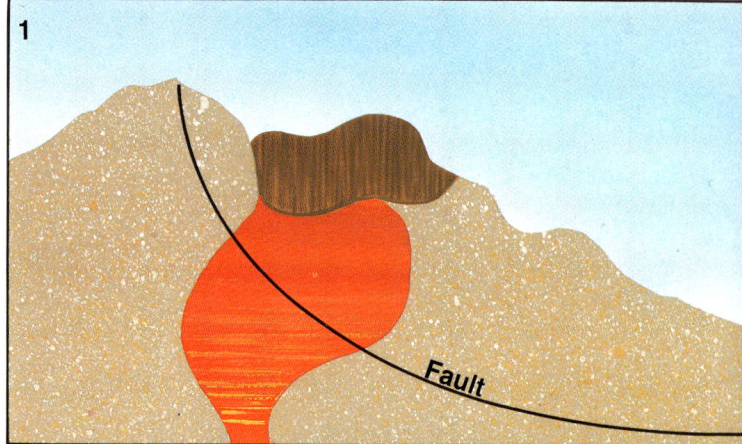

◄ Mount St Helens, in the state of Washington in the USA, is one of several active volcanoes in the Cascade Range. It erupted violently in May 1980.

Forecasting eruptions

Scientists measure changes in heat, pressure and temperature in volcanoes. They record tremors caused by rising magma and measure any swellings with an instrument called a tiltmeter. A tiltmeter works rather like a spirit level. In some countries, laser beams are used to measure swellings in the ground. Artificial satellites also keep watch on volcanoes and send back information. Forecasts are issued if an eruption is likely, so that people can be warned and leave the area as soon as possible.

◄ On 18 May 1980, an earthquake cracked the rocks at the top of Mount St Helens (1). The land above the fault slipped downhill. This released the pressure inside the volcano.

A surge of hot gases, followed by a cloud of hot ash shot sideways from the volcano (2), and raced downhill.

Black ash was exploded high into the air (3).

The surge of gases from Mount St Helens flattened trees over an area of 600 sq km. Black ash rained down from the sky. Scientists had forecast the eruption, but 60 people were killed. ►

Earthquakes

Earthquakes were once thought to be punishments for people who had offended gods. In Indonesia, one group of people made sacrifices to a god who, they believed, held up the Earth and so caused earthquakes. Myths also tried to explain why they occurred. A Mongolian story told how they were caused by a giant frog carrying the Earth on its back. Earthquakes were said to occur when the frog twitched.

We now know that earthquakes occur in several ways. Some are caused by explosions, landslides or volcanic eruptions. But most occur when rocks move along cracks or faults in the ground.

The greatest earthquakes occur around the edges of the moving plates, which are the biggest cracks in the Earth. Plate movements are not smooth. The edges of the plates are jagged and are usually jammed together. Finally, great pressure breaks the jam and the plates move in sudden jerks. These jerks cause earthquakes.

The 1755 earthquake which destroyed Lisbon, Portugal's capital, killed 60,000 people. Buildings collapsed and fires raged through the city. ▼

Great earthquakes

One of the most powerful earthquakes ever measured hit southern Alaska in 1964. The land shook for about seven minutes. Blocks of land were raised or lowered by up to 17 metres. Many buildings collapsed and cracks opened up in the ground. The earthquake also caused high sea waves called tsunamis. These waves probably killed most of the 115 people who died.

The San Francisco earthquake of 1906 killed more than 300 people and caused much damage. The earthquake started fires which raged through the city. It was caused by a sudden sideways movement along the San Andreas fault. Since 1906, many smaller earthquakes have occurred on the fault. Scientists think that another big earthquake is likely soon.

▲ An earthquake hit Lice in Turkey in 1975. More than 2,300 people were killed. Earthquakes are common in Turkey.

Earthquakes in Asia

The most destructive earthquakes have occurred in Asia. One in Japan in 1923 destroyed 575,000 homes. Another in China in 1556 killed about 800,000 people.

Forecasting earthquakes

Earthquakes are recorded at stations throughout the world. Scientists are seeking ways to forecast them. The Chinese have noticed that animals act strangely before an earthquake. Perhaps the animals can sense changes which we cannot. Chinese scientists also look for swellings in the ground where small tremors are taking place.

Such evidence was noted around the Chinese city of Haicheng in 1975. The people were told to leave the city just two hours before an earthquake destroyed it, and many lives were saved. But the Chinese were not able to predict several other earthquakes since 1975. In China, as elsewhere, scientists still have much to learn about earthquake forecasting.

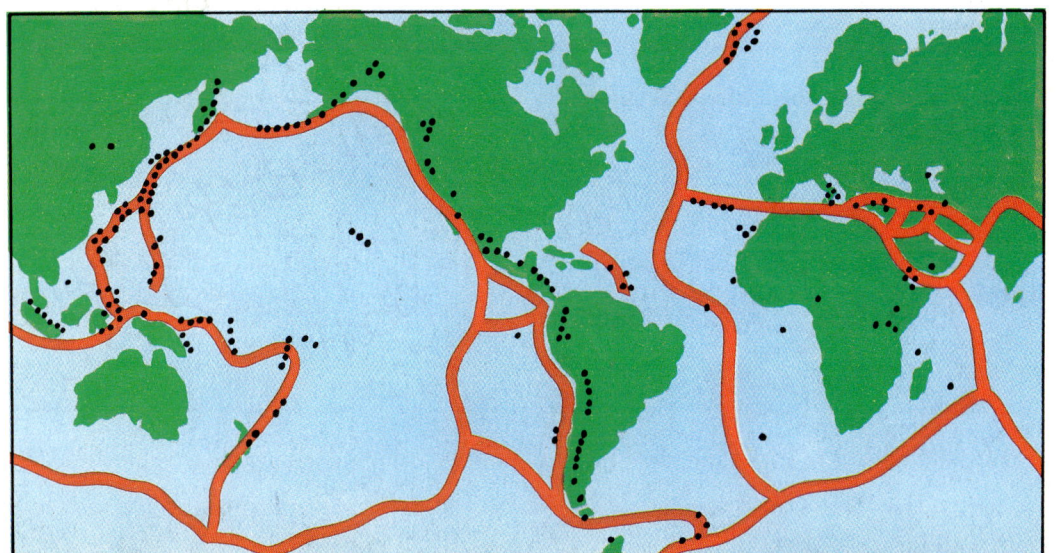

◄ The map shows the world's main earthquake and volcanic zones. They mainly follow the edges of the plates into which the Earth's crust is divided. The earthquake zones are shown in red and the volcanoes by black dots.

Mountain Building

Mountains were once dangerous places. They contained the hideouts of bandits who attacked travellers. They were also looked on as barriers between peoples, for example the Pyrenees mountains between the French and the Spanish. Until about 150 years ago, most people regarded them as mysterious places. The ancient Greeks thought that Mount Olympus, their highest peak, was the home of the gods. In East Africa, God lives on the top of Mount Kenya according to several local religions. Even today, many Japanese regard Mount Fuji as a holy mountain. Every year, thousands of Japanese make pilgrimages to a shrine on the top of Mount Fuji.

Different kinds of mountains

There are four main kinds of mountains: volcanic and dome mountains, fold mountains and block mountains. Volcanic eruptions have already been described on pages 24 and 25. Explosive volcanoes erupt hot ash into the air. They build up steep-sided cones of ash and other fragments of magma around the vent or openings. Other volcanoes, such as those in Hawaii, send out runny lava which flows a long way before it hardens. These volcanoes form flattened mountains, like up-turned saucers or shields. But most volcanic mountains consist of alternating layers of exploded fragments of magma and hardened lava.

Dome mountains

Dome mountains are formed by magma that does not reach the surface, but instead pushes the overlying rocks upwards. The Black Hills of South Dakota in the USA are dome mountains.

The world's highest mountain range is the Himalayas. It includes Mount Everest. Part of the Himalayas runs along the border between Nepal and China. ▶

Earth movements change the land. Flat layers of rock are folded by sideways pressure. Some blocks of land are pushed upwards between faults. These are called block mountains. Other blocks sink down between faults. They are called rift valleys. ▼

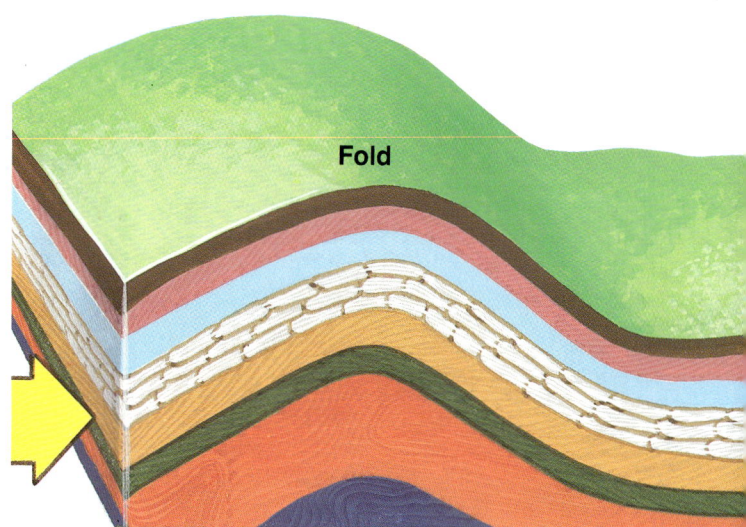

Fold

◄ The Sierra Nevada in California in the western USA is a high block mountain range.

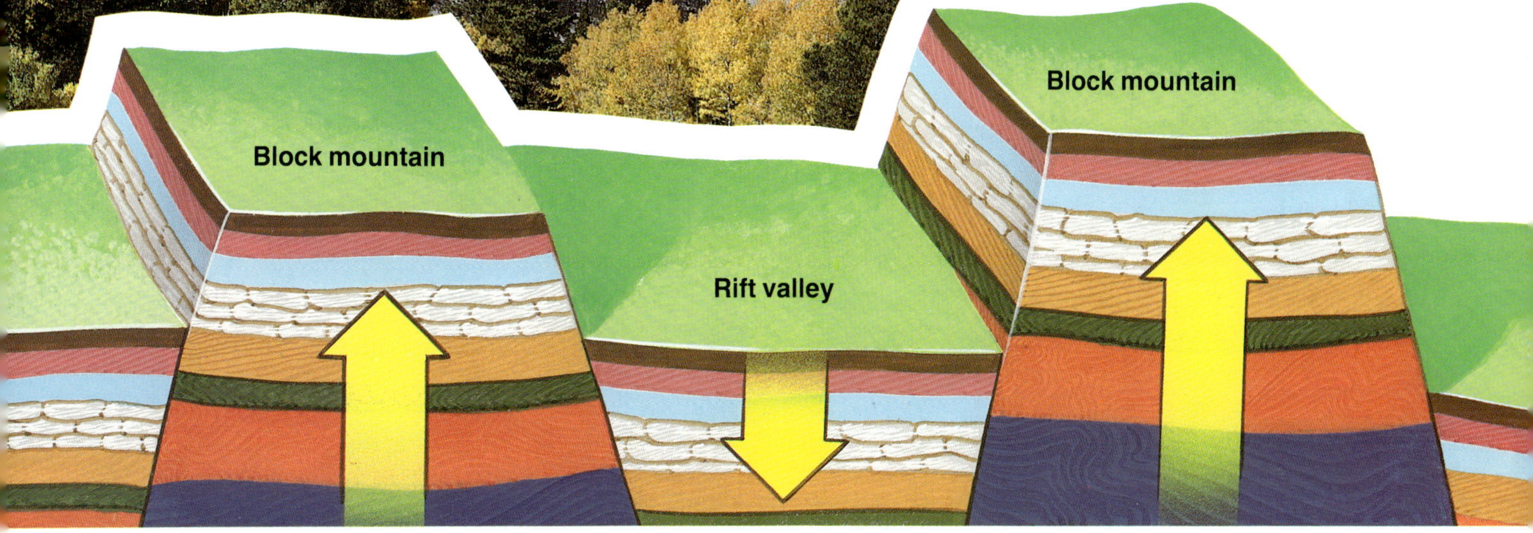

Block mountain

Block mountain

Rift valley

Fold mountains

Fold mountains are caused by sideways pressure. This buckles rock layers like a crumpled tablecloth. They form when two plates collide. The Himalayas began to rise when a plate carrying India pushed against a plate carrying Asia more than 50 million years ago. Between the plates was a sea. As the plates moved closer, the rocks on the sea bed were folded upwards. Later, the ocean vanished and India was joined to Asia. The rocks on the old sea bed now formed high mountains. The Alps in Europe are fold mountains formed in a similar way.

Block mountains

Plate movements pull and stretch rocks which are some distance away from plate edges. This cracks the rocks and produces faults. Some blocks of land sink down between faults to form deep valleys. The East African Rift Valley was formed in this way.

Other blocks are pushed up between faults. They become block mountains. Examples include the Sierra Nevada in the western USA and the Ruwenzori Mountains of East Africa.

On Christmas Day, 1974, a tropical cyclone (or hurricane) hit Darwin, the capital city of Australia's Northern Territory.

WEATHER

We have seen some of the ways the weather slowly alters the Earth. The weather too is constantly changing. A thin blanket of air, called the atmosphere, surrounds the Earth. The atmosphere is changing all the time, because of winds and the Sun's heat. Weather is the state of the atmosphere at a certain time. It may change from hour to hour. The climate of a place is the average, or usual, weather. Climates also change. Only 15,000 years ago, world climates were unlike those of today. Much of the northern hemisphere was in the grip of the Ice Age.

Weather and climate affect our daily lives. Rain can stop sporting events and fog can bring traffic to a standstill. Even worse, people may starve when droughts cause crop failures. The studies of weather and climate and weather forecasting are now extremely important.

People have always been interested in the weather. In China, people once thought that Mother-Lightning produced flashes of lightning with a mirror, while the Master of Rain used his sword to sprinkle water over the Earth from a pot which he carried. The Plains Indians of North America thought that thunder was the voice of the Great Spirit (Supreme Being). Tlaloc, a Mexican rain god, was worshipped by the people. Tlaloc had four pots. One held water that made plants grow. The water in another caused plant diseases. A third had water that turned into frost and the fourth destroyed fruit. The Mexicans made human sacrifices to Tlaloc to keep him happy.

◄ People in south-eastern Asia are happy when the yearly monsoon rains arrive, because these rains will make the crops grow. Children shelter under home-made umbrellas.

Weather Forecasting

The Sun may be shining when we get out of bed, but we may still want to know whether it will rain later in the day. People once used simple methods of weather forecasting. Some hung up seaweed in their gardens. If the seaweed was dry, then the weather would stay fine. But when there is a lot of moisture in the air, the seaweed absorbs some of it and feels wet. This shows that rain may be on the way.

There are many old sayings about the weather. One says: 'Red sky at night, shepherds' delight. Red sky in the morning, shepherds' warning'. This means that a red sky at sunset will be followed by a fine day. But a red sky in the early morning means that rain is likely.

There is some truth in this and many other old sayings. But today we turn to the radio, television or the morning newspaper for a more accurate weather forecast.

Weather forecasts are important not just to help us to decide whether we need a raincoat. Ships' captains are interested in gales and hurricanes, and airline pilots need information about fog, clouds and wind speeds.

Collecting information

There are weather stations all over the world, on land and at sea. At these stations, weather conditions are measured regularly every three or six hours.

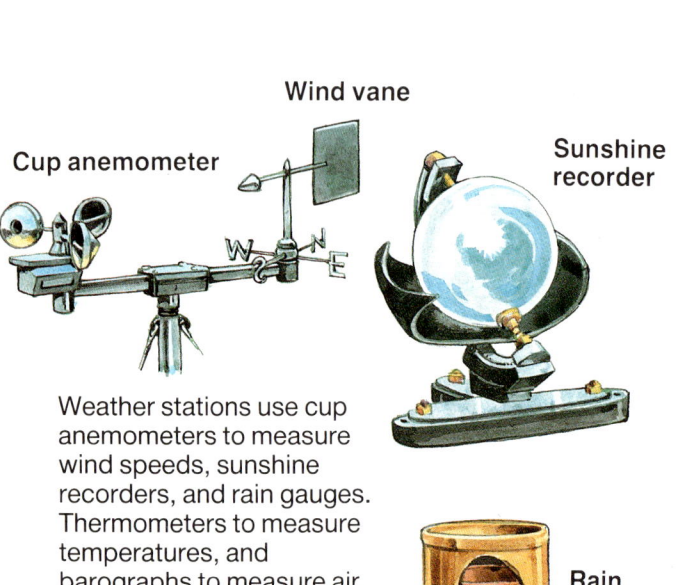

Cup anemometer **Wind vane** **Sunshine recorder**

Weather stations use cup anemometers to measure wind speeds, sunshine recorders, and rain gauges. Thermometers to measure temperatures, and barographs to measure air pressure, are kept in a special box, called a Stevenson Screen.

Rain gauge

Stevenson screen

Thermometers

Barograph

◄ Photographs of cloud formations taken by spacecraft and artificial satellites are used by weather forecasters.

Measurements are made of the air pressure, temperature and humidity, or moistness of the air. Wind speeds and directions, the amount of rain and snow, the hours of sunshine, the visibility (how far one can see), and the height and type of clouds are also recorded.

Conditions higher in the atmosphere are measured by sending up balloons. Attached to the balloons are instruments that measure pressure, temperature and humidity at various heights. A radio transmitter automatically relays this information back to a receiver on the ground. When all the measurements are complete, they are put into code and sent to a weather centre.

Preparing weather forecasts
At the weather centres, information from nearby stations is collected. Some information also comes from satellite photographs which show cloud formations over the Earth. Satellites are also used to track hurricanes, so that people are warned of their approach.

At many stations, the information is processed by a computer. The computer produces simple weather maps which summarize all the information at ground level and at higher levels in the atmosphere.

Weather scientists called meteorologists study these maps and work out how the weather has changed in the last few hours. This gives them an idea of how the weather will change over the next day. They draw maps of what they think the weather will be like in 12, 24 and 36 hours time. From their maps, they prepare written forecasts and send them to newspapers and radio and television stations.

Computing forecasts
Computers are used to speed up the preparation of weather forecasts. But computers don't have the knowledge and experience about local conditions that meteorologists have. Meteorologists are still vitally important in making accurate weather forecasts.

Changing Climates

About 140 years ago, a Swiss naturalist, Louis Agassiz studied the rocks in the Alps. He wanted to know how glaciers changed the land. Later, he left Switzerland and travelled in Europe and North America. There he found many ice-worn rocks and ice-carved features in lowlands which had mild, warm weather. Agassiz realized that this proved that ice had once covered much of Europe and northern America.

The Ice Age began about 1.75 million years ago and began to end about 12,000 years ago. It was not cold all the time in the Ice Age. There were times when it was warmer than today and tropical forest grew in parts of the northern continents which are too cold today for such plants.

During the warm periods hippopotamuses and lions lived in Europe. In cold periods, ice sheets spread south. Only animals with warm coats, such as woolly mammoths, could live near the ice. We know where these animals lived, because their fossils are found in rocks.

In the Ice Age, which ended about 12,000 years ago, ice covered much of northern Europe and North America. Woolly rhinoceroses and woolly mammoths roamed the land.

◄ A glacier carried this boulder to its place in the Yosemite Valley in the Sierra Nevada mountains in California, USA, during the Ice Age.

Other climatic changes

The study of fossils shows that climates have changed many times in Earth history. For example, coal seams have been found in the icy continent of Antarctica. Coal is formed from plants which grow in warm swamps. Such plants could not grow in Antarctica today.

Geologists have also found evidence in the rocks of another Ice Age, around 300 million years ago. This affected southern America, southern Africa, India, western Australia and Antarctica. Continental drift may explain such mysteries. Antarctica was probably much farther north when the coal was formed. And the southern continents were probably grouped around the South Pole 300 million years ago.

Recent changes

Continental drift is slow and cannot explain the last Ice Age or other recent changes. For example, a 'Little Ice Age' occurred in Europe, reaching its peak in the 17th century. You can see evidence of this in some 17th century European paintings. Often the rivers, such as the Thames in London, are completely frozen. But now they never freeze over.

Today some scientists think that a new Ice Age may be on the way. But no one can prove this. Why do these changes occur? The dust from volcanic eruptions may cause some changes. It can block out sunlight and so cool the Earth's surface. Big eruptions may cause cold weather for several years. Other reasons are linked with the changes in the Earth's orbit around the Sun and the tilt of its axis. The Earth's axis is the imaginary line joining the North and South Poles. It is possible that over thousands of years such changes make climates vary on Earth.

▲ Cave paintings of people with grazing animals are found in the Sahara. This hot desert was a grassland in the Ice Age.

LIFE ON EARTH

The variety of plant and animal life on our planet is quite tremendous. The main reason for this is the climate. Some places are hot and some cold, some are dry and some are wet. The hottest places on Earth are in the tropics, north and south of the Equator. The coldest places are near the North and South Poles. Between them, in both the northern and southern hemispheres, are a series of climatic zones. All the areas within one zone have a similar climate, with similar plants and animals.

Plants and animals are adapted to the climate of the region in which they live. For example, the polar bear in the Arctic is kept warm by its thick coat. South of the Arctic in the northern hemisphere is a region called the tundra. In the short summer, the snow melts and plants such as mosses and lichens grow. But it is too cold and windy for trees to grow. Some animals, such as reindeer, graze on the tundra in summer. In winter, they seek shelter in the northern forests of such trees as fir, pine and spruce. These trees are coniferous or evergreen trees. Bears, moose and wolves live here too.

Temperate or mild, moist regions have many deciduous trees. These are trees which shed their leaves in winter, like ash and oak. Deciduous forests once covered much of western Europe and the eastern USA. But most of them have been cut down now to make way for farmland.

The tropics include wet places with thick rain forests. Most animals, including monkeys, live in the trees. The tropics also contain areas called savannas with a long dry season. Grassland with scattered trees covers these areas. In Africa, many animals roam the savanna, including elephants, giraffes, rhinoceroses and zebras. The hot tropical deserts have specially adapted plants. For example, cacti store water. One desert animal, the camel, can go for days without water. But when it is thirsty, it can gulp down 130 litres in 10 minutes.

Mountains have many climates, because the higher you go the colder it gets. Even on the Equator, there are snow-capped mountains. Below the snow is a tundra zone. Lower still are grass and forest zones.

The climate determines the plants and animals of any region. But people can go anywhere. They can live in air-conditioned homes in the hot tropics. They can also live in ice-bound Antarctica in heated homes. But in Antarctica they must get all their supplies from outside.

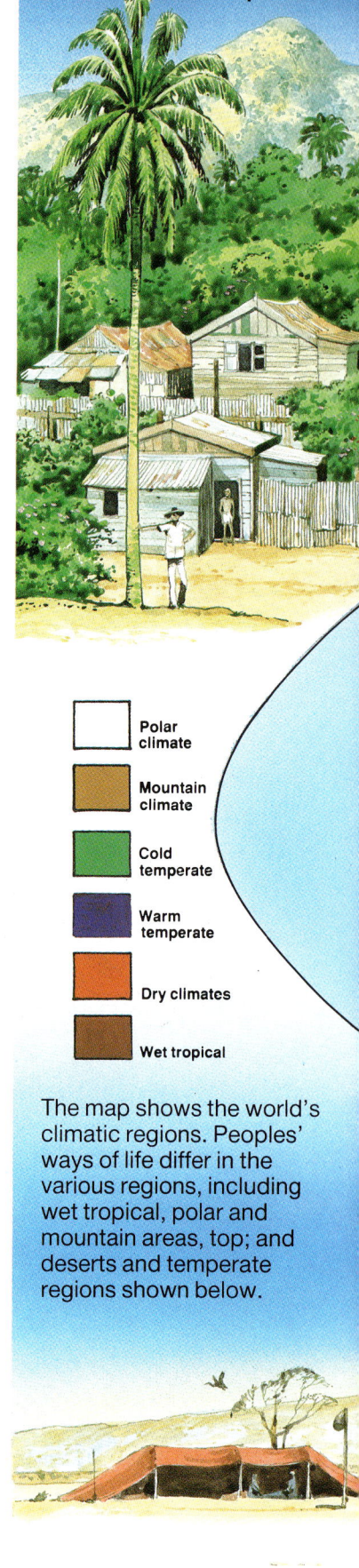

Wet tropical clima

Polar climate

Mountain climate

Cold temperate

Warm temperate

Dry climates

Wet tropical

The map shows the world's climatic regions. Peoples' ways of life differ in the various regions, including wet tropical, polar and mountain areas, top; and deserts and temperate regions shown below.

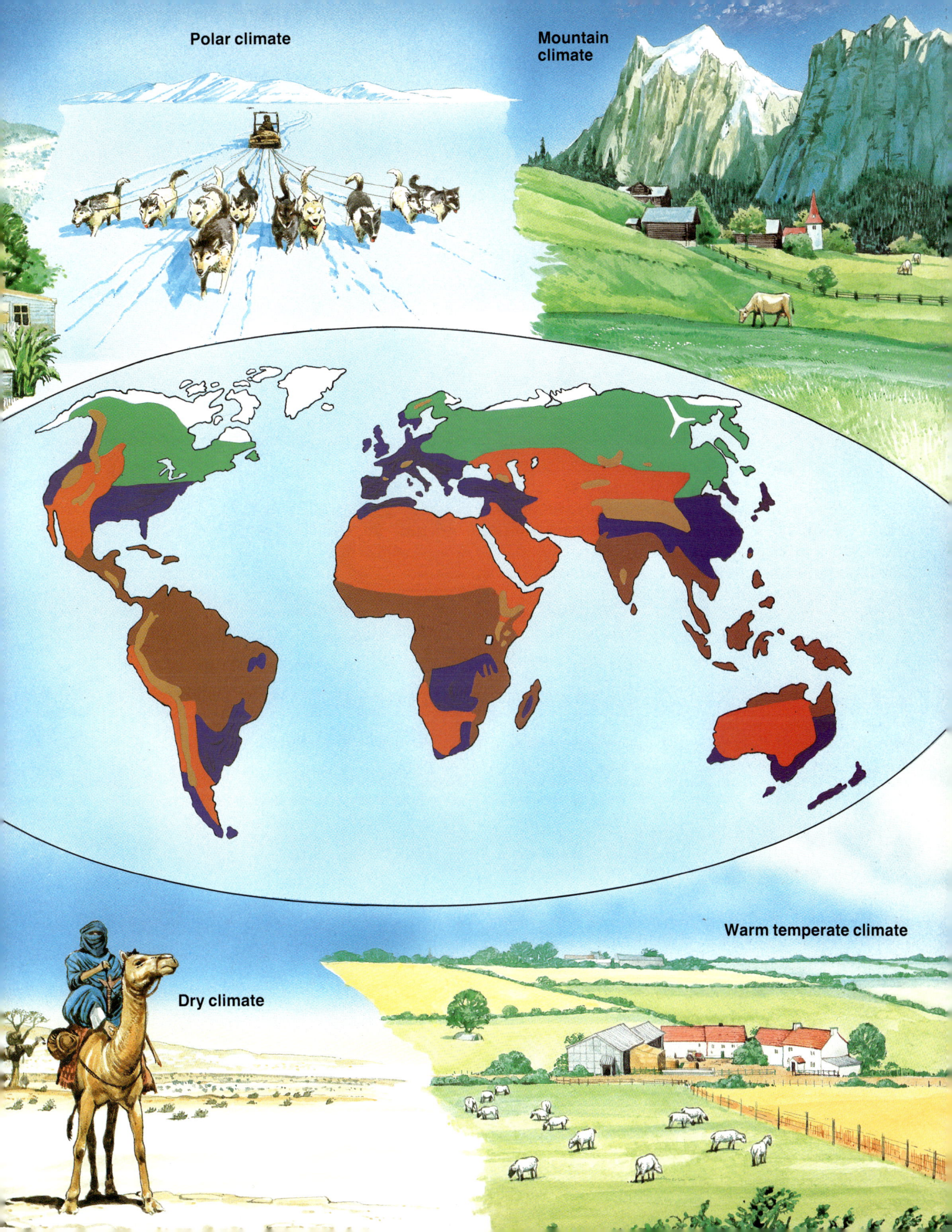

Polar climate

Mountain climate

Dry climate

Warm temperate climate

Interfering with Nature

In nature, living things depend upon each other. For animals to survive, there must be enough food for them to eat. If the food supply is reduced, then the number of animals will decrease. Some animals may even become extinct.

The dependence of living things on each other is called the 'balance of nature'. The science which studies plants and animals, how they live together and how they are affected by their environment or surroundings is called ecology. Ecologists also study how people change environments and upset the balance of nature.

Damaging the land
Some of the farmers who settled on the Great Plains of the USA about 120 years ago ploughed the land to grow crops. They removed the grass which bound the soil together. During droughts, the wind started to blow away the dry, exposed soil. Several droughts in the 1920s turned large areas into 'dust bowls' or deserts.

Deserts are now being created in Africa. There, the Sahara is moving south by 100 metres a year in places. On the edge of the desert, a dry grassy region called the Sahel, has been overgrazed by large herds of livestock. The grass has been eaten away and long droughts have stopped new growth. Millions of cattle have died as the Sahara has spread south. Their owners and their families have starved to death.

Other threatened regions are the rain forests of South America, Africa and Asia. These forests are being cut down to make way for farms, mines, roads and factories. As the rain forests disappear, so also do plants and animals. Sadly, scientists have never studied or even named many of these plants and animals.

Some of the ways we pollute the air, water and the land.

▲ A tree crusher is clearing forest in the Amazon basin of Peru. The world's rain forests are vanishing quickly, at a rate of 50 hectares a minute.

Destroying a way of life

The Indians in the rain forests of South America are also threatened. By clearing the forests, people are taking away the Indians' land and so destroying their whole way of life. For thousands of years, the Indians have been able to live in harmony with the forest, without destroying it. Now some people fear that unless the Indians' interests are protected, they may not survive beyond the next two or three generations.

Pollution

People misuse the Earth in other ways. In cities, chimneys pour gases and smoke into the air. Factories pump poisonous wastes into rivers and seas and other wastes are dumped on land. These are some examples of pollution.

▲ As South America's forests disappear, the Indians who live there are losing their lands, traditions and culture.

Pollution occurred when a spray called DDT was used on crops to kill insects. The DDT not only killed the insects, but also the birds and other animals which ate the insects. DDT is now banned in some countries. But other harmful chemicals are still being used. Sometimes not enough precautions are taken when they are produced. For example in 1984 over 2,000 people died in Bhopal, India, when poisonous gas leaked from a chemical factory into the homes near the factory. The deadly gas also badly injured the eyes and lungs of over 200,000 people.

Looking after our Planet

Solar panels

We have learned in recent years of the many ways in which people have been harming our planet. Scientists have also worked hard to find ways of putting things right and stopping even more damage. They have found ways of farming the land without destroying the soil, through the use of fertilizers, contour ploughing and crop rotation. Even dry grasslands can be farmed without turning them into deserts. But sometimes these new methods are too costly for the poor farmers in the world who really need them. New methods may also go against old customs. In the Sahel, people do not want to cut the size of their herds. This is because the number of cattle they own determines their importance in society.

Controlling pollution
People living around Minamata Bay in Japan in the early 1950s started to fall ill. Many of them died. Everyone wanted to know what was causing the terrible illness. Scientists found that factory wastes were being pumped into the bay. Fish in the water were absorbing the poison in the wastes. The fishermen and their families who ate these fish were falling ill. Once the reasons for the illness were understood, the factory was not allowed to pump wastes into the bay.

Scientists have explained the effects of many other kinds of pollution. For example, about 4,000 people died of chest illnesses during a severe smog in London in 1952. Smog is smoke from factory chimneys mixed with fog. The smog was the cause of the deaths. Britain made a law in 1956 which made factories and homes use smokeless fuels. Since then, smog has not occurred in London. But there are some types of pollution which are still only partly understood. Sometimes, too, governments are slow to pass laws to stop pollution.

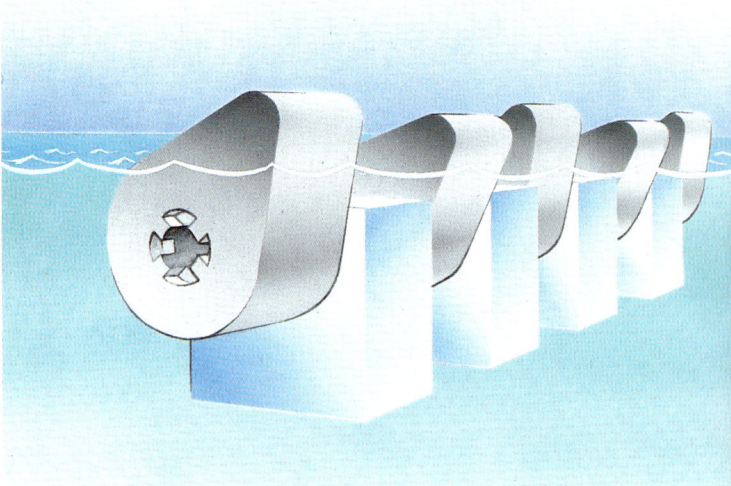
Moving floats in the sea

Conserving our resources
The Earth is a storehouse of riches. It provides us with fuels, metals and stone from the Earth's crust, wood and crops from the land. The demand for all these things is increasing.

In order that enough food is grown for the increasing population of the world, new farmland has to be found. For example, the Dutch have pushed back the sea by building strong walls. The land behind the walls is then farmed. In many deserts, water is piped in from far away and used to irrigate the land. Former deserts can now produce crops. These are examples of how we can reclaim the land.

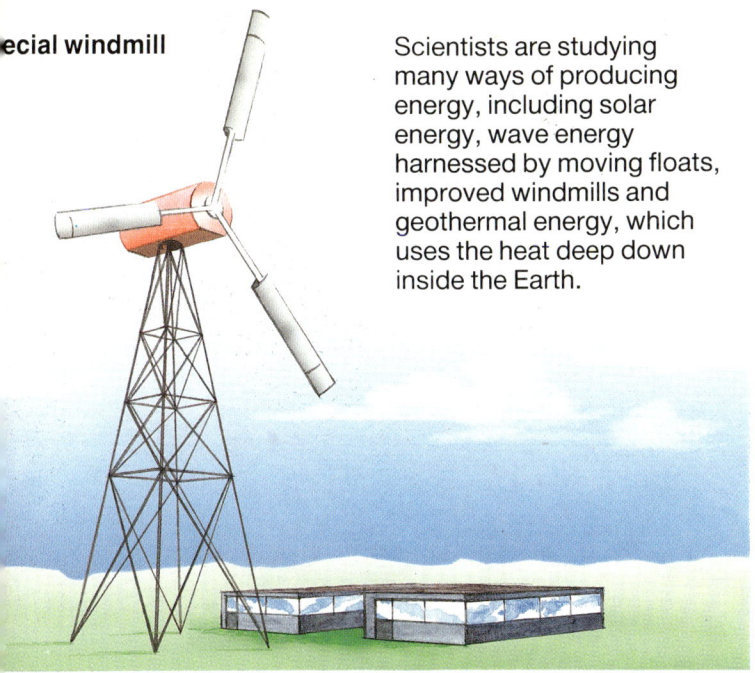

ecial windmill

Scientists are studying many ways of producing energy, including solar energy, wave energy harnessed by moving floats, improved windmills and geothermal energy, which uses the heat deep down inside the Earth.

▲ Dry parts of the world can become rich farmland with irrigation. These round irrigated fields are in Colorado, USA.

othermal energy

The people of the world also need increasing amounts of minerals and fuels. Some, such as iron ore, are common and abundant. Others, such as oil and natural gas, will run out one day. Scientists are now studying other ways of producing energy for the time when the oil and gas run out. Some methods are shown above.

Today it is more important than ever that we look after our planet. Governments are slowly starting to take action together. Individuals can help too. For instance some volunteers clean areas that have already been harmed by pollution. In different ways we can all make sure that the Earth will be fit for future generations.

▲ Here volunteers are helping to improve their environment by cleaning rubbish from a canal. Old canals can then be used for leisure activities.

Books and Places

Books to read

Geology, D. Dixon, Franklin Watts, 1979*
Children's Encyclopedia of Our World, Usborne Publishing, 1979*
Rivers and Lakes, K. Lye, Macdonald Educational, 1980
Mountains, R. Woodcock, Macdonald Educational, 1980
Deserts, P. Monahan, Macdonald Educational, 1979
Oceans, J. Parsons, Macdonald Educational, 1979
Fossils, M. Lambert, Ward Lock, 1978
The Observer's Guide to Geology, I. O. Evans, Frederick Warne, 1979
Minerals and Rocks, K. Lye, Ward Lock, 1979
Hunting the Past, L. B. Halstead, Hamish Hamilton, 1982
Nature's Roundabout, P. Armstrong, Ladybird Books, 1979
*(Out of print, but available from libraries.)

Places to visit

Many local museums, even in small towns, often contain information and exhibits concerning the geology of the area. But the major museums are in the cities. In London, the Geological Museum and the British Museum (Natural History) are among the world's best.

The Geological Museum has permanent exhibitions on 'The Story of the Earth', 'British Fossils', 'Britain before Man' and 'Treasures of the Earth'. The Geological Museum publishes the following booklets:
The Story of the Earth
Earthquakes
Volcanoes
The Age of the Earth
Britain before Man.
These inexpensive booklets are written for adults. But they contain many superb and fascinating illustrations.

The British Museum (Natural History) has wonderful displays of fossils, including huge dinosaurs, mammals, fishes, plants and so on. It also publishes excellent books on British fossils.

Most of Britain's leading cities have fine museums with much of interest concerning our changing Earth. For example, the cities of Bristol, Cardiff, Dudley, Leicester, Liverpool and Manchester all have interesting museums.

In Europe, North America and Australasia, the situation is similar. If you are on holiday, visit the local museum and you will almost certainly find some information on the local geology, along with displays of fossils.

In the USA, the great museums include the American Museum of Natural History, New York City; the Field Museum of Natural History, Chicago; the Carnegie Museum, Pittsburgh; and the National Museum of Natural History (which is part of the Smithsonian Institution) in Washington DC.

◄ The Dead Sea is so salty that you can read a newspaper without sinking.

Salto Angel in Venezuela, South America, is the world's highest waterfall. ▶

Indonesia, in south-east Asia, has more volcanoes (167) than any other country.
Lake Baykal, in the USSR, is the world's deepest lake (1,940 metres).
Lake Superior is the world's biggest fresh water lake. It is one of the Great Lakes on the USA-Canada border.
Lambert Glacier, in Antarctica, is the world's longest glacier. It is more than 500 km long.
Mariana Trench, in the western Pacific Ocean, has the deepest point in the oceans. It is about 11 km deep.
Mount Everest, on the Nepal-China border in the Himalayan range, is the world's highest mountain. It rises 8,848 metres above sea level.
Nile River, in north-eastern Africa, is the world's longest river. It flows for 6,670 km.
Sahara, in North Africa, is the world's largest desert. It covers 8.4 million sq km.
Salto Angel (Angel Falls), in Venezuela, is the world's highest waterfall. It drops 979 metres.
Vostok station, Antarctica, recorded the world's lowest screen temperature (−89.2°C) in 1983.

Word list

Arctic The area around the North Pole, north of the Arctic Circle, or about 66½° North latitude.

Caves Hollows in the ground. There are sea caves, lava caves and ice caves, but the largest are those caves which form in the rock limestone.

Continental drift The name for the theory which says that the continents are moved around by currents in the upper part of the Earth's mantle.

Core The Earth's core measures about 6,920 km across. It is solid in the centre. The outer core is probably liquid.

Crust The thin, solid outer covering of the Earth. The ocean crust averages about 6 km in thickness. The continental crust reaches a maximum depth of 60 to 70 km under high mountains.

Delta An area of land at the mouths of some rivers made of sediment dropped there by the river.

Epoch A division of time in Earth history. Several epochs make up a period.

Equator The imaginary line around the Earth exactly half way between the North and South Poles.

Estuary The part of a river's mouth which is affected by the tides.

Era The longest of the time spans into which Earth history is divided.

Extinction The complete disappearance of a plant or animal species.

Fault A break or crack in rocks, along which the rocks have moved.

Hemisphere Half a sphere. The northern hemisphere includes the land and sea north of the Equator.

Ice Ages Ages in Earth history when ice sheets spread over large areas which are now ice-free.

Igneous rock Rock formed from molten magma. The word igneous comes from the Latin word for fire.

Land reclamation Turning useless land, such as deserts, into farmland.

Latitude The distance of a point on the Earth's surface from the Equator. It is measured in degrees. The North Pole is 90° latitude and the Equator is 0° latitude.

Magma Molten material which cools underground or on the surface to form igneous rocks.

Mantle The part of the Earth between the crust and the core. It is about 2,900 km thick.

Metamorphic rock Igneous or sedimentary rock that has been changed by great heat or enormous pressure inside the Earth.

Period A division of time in Earth history. Several periods make one era.

Plates Sections of the Earth, consisting of the crust and part of the upper mantle. Plates are moved around by currents in the mantle.

Poles The two points at the end of the Earth's axis.

Sedimentary rocks Rocks formed by chemical processes or from sediments of worn rock, or the remains of once-living things.

Seismology The study of earthquakes.

Solar System The Sun, the planets and their moons, asteroids (small planets), comets and meteors that revolve around the Sun make up the Solar System.

Tropics The land between latitude 23°27′ North (the Tropic of Cancer) and 23°27′ South (the Tropic of Capricorn).

Tundra The treeless zone bordering the icy Arctic lands. Tundra occurs only in the northern hemisphere.

Volcano A vent, or hole, in the ground through which magma is ejected. The word volcano is also used for mountains formed from lava and ash.

Water vapour Invisible moisture in the air.